Baby Owner's Manual

Baby Owner's Manual

What to Expect and
How to Survive the First Year

THIRD EDITION

Edward R. Christophersen

Westport Publishers, Inc.
Kansas City, Missouri

ISBN 0-933701-31-4

Cover photography: Eli Reichman
Cover art: Network Graphics

Text photography: Edward R. Christophersen, Clark H. Smith
Text art: Network Graphics

Baby on cover: Noah H. Butler-Smith

Library of Congress Cataloging-in-Publication Data

Christophersen, Edward R.
    Baby owner's manual.

    1. Infants—Care. I. Title.
RJ61.C5527   1988   649'.122   88-20843
ISBN 0-933701-31-4 (pbk.)

Printed in the United States of America

Contents

Preface

The *Baby Owner's Manual* was written for expectant parents and first-time parents. The topics covered include those that parents ask about (or worse, don't ask about) most frequently. It is not a self-help manual any more than the manual that you received with your last car was a self-help manual. Nor was it written for parents who have problems infants. This manual assumes that you have a fairly good idea of when your baby's diaper needs changing, just as a Chevrolet owner's manual assumes that you know to use your headlights at night and to roll up the car windows when it begins to rain outside.

With virtually every major purchase that you make, you receive an owner's or operator's manual. Yet, when you have a baby, you receive little or no instruction on what to expect and how to care for your baby. Many maternity nurses set aside some time for new moms while they are in the hospital to teach them some of the basics about their babies. The nurses can't possibly teach the moms about everything that happens to a baby during the first year. The moms hope that the rest will come naturally. Compare this to the five or ten minutes that a car salesperson spends with you when you purchase a new automobile to show you how to operate the features on your car. When new car buyers get their car home, most of them will sit down and read the owner's manual carefully and they may discover some subtle points about their new car that were previously unknown to them.

Fortunately, as far as standard equipment is concerned, children are about the same. The *Baby Owner's Manual* recognizes that having a baby is not as easy as purchasing a new car;

it gives new parents a quick and easy reference, presented in a humorous and easy-to-understand manner, to allay the fears and anxieties of having a new baby.

The third edition of *Baby Owner's Manual* has given me the opportunity to add a lot of material that wasn't in the earlier editions—material that should provide you with much more information about your baby.

The main reason for writing *Baby Owner's Manual* is my family. I share so much enjoyment with my son, Hunter, my daughter, Cathy, and my wife, Miki, that I want other parents to have as much pleasure as I am having. Fathers often miss out on a lot of the fun of having a new baby. Infants and children are delightful, curious, challenging, and rewarding. They deserve every opportunity we can provide so we can help them realize their fullest potential.

Acknowledgments

The motivation for writing this book came from my two children, Hunter and Catherine. They, along with their mother, Miki, have taught me so much about love, understanding, and caring. The actual book would never have been completed without the able assistance of Barbara Cochrane and Jane Doyle Guthrie.

A special thanks is due to the babies who appear in the pictures throughout this book: Elizabeth, C.J., Meghan, Nathan, Alexander, Diane, Spencer, and Katie. Although they will have to wait many years before my "Thank You" means anything to them, I am grateful that their parents consented to allow me to photograph them and to include their photographs in this book.

Edward R. Christophersen
July 1988

The Madison Avenue Baby

If you look at the pictures of babies on boxes of disposable diapers, or jars of baby food, or on the covers of parents' magazines, you will find an artifact of American life. These babies are clean, quiet, happy, and well groomed, and they do not look like they need to have their diapers changed. This image of the typical American baby tends to mislead parents into thinking that they will have that kind of baby.

Unfortunately, very few parents actually get the kind of baby that is so heavily marketed by Madison Avenue. Most babies spend a couple of minutes out of every day acting like a "Perfect Baby" (usually while sleeping); the rest of the time they act like normal babies.

Many people like to use special words to refer to what babies do. When a baby happens to have a little air in his stomach, his parents work hard to get him to "bubble." He is held

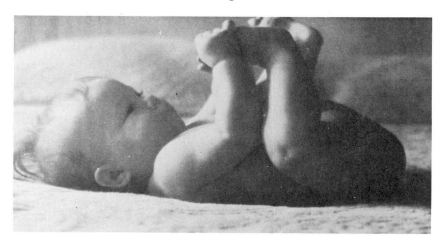

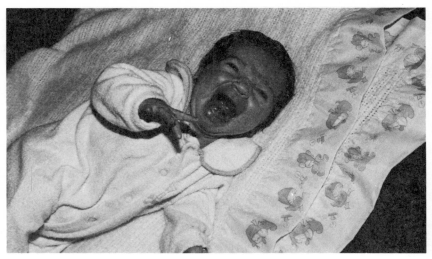

A real baby

over his parent's shoulder, jiggled, and patted on the back. When he finally releases the air, he is congratulated for doing so. However, when an adult allows air to escape from his stomach, it is called "belching" and everyone around the offender is embarrassed, although the same type of gas exited in the same way. Isn't it odd that it's an accomplishment for a baby and a source of reprimand for an adult?

Similarly, babies "spit up," while adults "vomit," "puke," or "throw up." In both cases the partial contents of the stomach are expelled through the mouth. Yet, for the baby this is acceptable; for the adult, no way! New parents somehow expect something different because the words are different. After a new parent has changed enough soiled diapers, cleaned up enough spit-up, and gotten up enough bubbles, he will know that, while these certainly are not difficult tasks, they are not quite as pleasant as the people on Madison Avenue purport. You probably are going to have a baby who cries when she needs something and who does not always look clean or feel happy. You are going to have a real baby.

While You're Still in the Hospital

Most mothers and fathers instinctively count their baby's fingers and toes; this act seems to be secondary only to establishing whether their baby is a boy or a girl. This is just fine, but you will discover more about your baby if you explore what he already knows. You will probably be very surprised! The exercises described will help to teach you a lot about your baby and how he responds to you and to what you do. Begin them when your baby is awake and does not need anything. Waiting may be hard, but it's worth it.

Hearing

You can follow a simple procedure to explore your baby's hearing. Hold your baby firmly in front of you with her head to

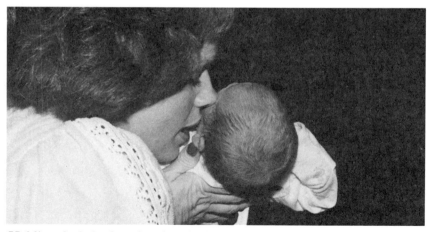

Holding the baby for a hearing check-up

your right and her feet to your left. Hold her slightly above the level of your chin. Say her name in a normal voice tone and volume. Do not act as though your baby is hearing-impaired or your voice will startle her. When you talk she will turn her head slowly toward the direction of your voice. Then, to assure yourself that she is actually turning toward your voice, try this test in the other direction. That is, turn your baby around so that her head is on your left and her feet are on your right. Many new parents are surprised to learn how well their new baby can hear.

Vision

You can also explore your baby's vision. Hold your baby securely in front of you, so that his face is directly opposite yours and about ten to twelve inches away. Look directly into his eyes. You will notice that his eyes rove around. As soon as his eyes are focused directly on your face, begin talking to him,

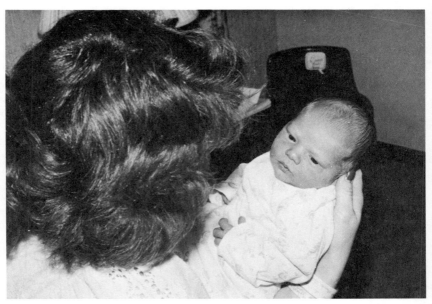

Holding the baby for a vision check-up

perhaps saying his name, as you slowly and deliberately move your face from one side to the other. After you have practiced this several times, you will find that your baby will follow your face part of the time. In so doing, you are establishing that your baby has functional sight at this very young age. Most infants who are one or two days old can follow their caregiver's face as it moves left and right. If your baby can follow your face both ways, then check to see if he can follow it when you move your face up and down in front of him. This requires a little more skill on your part because you have to be able to hold your baby still while you move your face up above his face and down below his face. For another test, determine if your baby can follow your face as you move it in a small circle around his face.

Remember, none of these exercises are meaningful unless you begin when the baby's eyes focused on your face. If you start to move your face in any direction and the baby does not follow it, he probably was not focused on your face when you started the test.

Both of the exercises on hearing and vision are designed to show you what your newborn can do rather than to test her senses. If you ever have doubts about your baby's senses, contact the doctor who normally takes care of your baby.

Self-Quieting Skills

As babies differ in the color of their eyes and the color of their hair, they differ in their ability to calm themselves after they have started crying. Some babies are incredibly adept at quieting themselves; others have a lot of trouble doing so. The procedure for checking your baby's self-quieting skills is a little more difficult than the procedure for vision or hearing, but it isn't hard to do.

Begin the procedure shortly after your baby's last feeding so he won't be hungry. If he is hungry and fussy when you try this exercise, it will be meaningless because he will not calm down until he is fed. Without picking him up, move him around in his bassinet, so that he begins crying. Leave him completely alone and observe how he quiets himself. It is important that you don't step in immediately to help him, or you'll never know what kinds of skills he was born with for self-quieting.

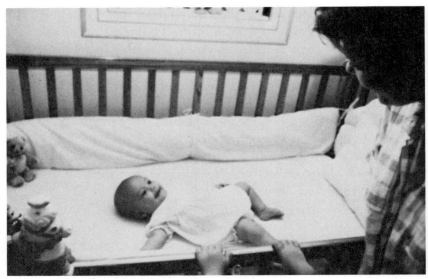

Talking softly to the baby

If he hasn't quieted himself after a minute or two (those minutes do seem like hours to a new parent!), then position your face about ten to twelve inches above his head and say his name in a normal voice. Talk to him for a minute, say his name, and see if he can quiet himself with only your voice for help. If this doesn't work, put one of your hands over one of his hands and hold them to his chest firmly and talk to him. If this doesn't work after a minute or two, pick him up. Hold him close to your chest and talk to him while you rock him gently from side to side. If none of these steps work, then securely wrap him in a receiving blanket, hold him firmly to your chest, and rock him gently while talking to him. This last step usually works with most infants.

During the first couple of weeks of life, babies commonly exhibit a Moro reflex or response when they are startled or stimulated dramatically and their whole body jumps. Their arms and legs suddenly jerk at the same time. When their nervous system matures, the Moro reflex will no longer appear when they are startled. Even though an infant exhibits the Moro reflex for a second or two, it can scare a new parent who wasn't expecting it. Your baby may cry after he exhibits the Moro reflex.

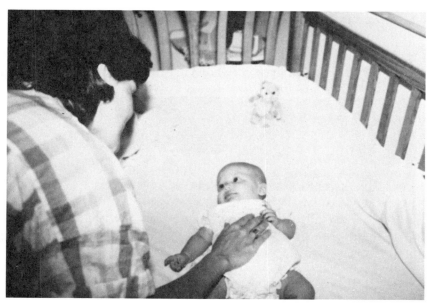

Helping the baby to quiet

If you find that your baby has a difficult time quieting himself when he is three or four days old, don't be discouraged. Wait another week or two and try the series of exercises again, making sure you give him enough time to self-quiet at each step before moving to the next step. You should assess his self-quieting skills periodically during the first month of life so that you will know when you need to help him self-quiet and when you can be assured that he will be all right in a minute. Remember, a baby is born with a self-quieting ability; it has nothing to do with the kind of parent you are. It is simply one measure of your baby's ability to mobilize innate skills to cope with his surroundings.

Infants differ greatly in their ability to quiet themselves. But, unless you try these self-quieting exercises several times and give your baby an adequate amount of time to quiet himself, you will never know how good his skills really are. Some infants can quiet themselves from a full scream to almost a sleeping state in less than one minute, whereas other infants require a great deal of help from a caregiver before they can be quieted. One thing you can be assured of—whether your baby is very easy to quiet or very hard to quiet when he's two or three

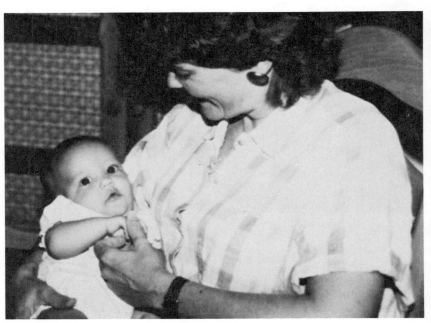

A calm baby

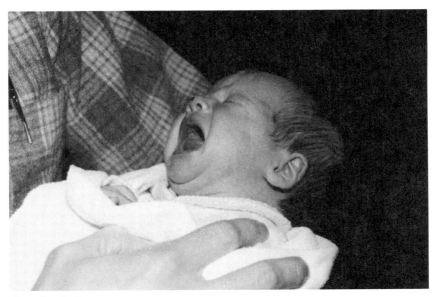

A crying baby

days old certainly is not due to something you have done. Rather, his ability to self-quiet is part of his disposition and something you will have to learn to tolerate. If you find that your baby has few self-quieting skills, then most of the suggestions for relief that you receive from your well-intentioned friends may not work with your baby. If their suggestions do not work when you try them, you may become more discouraged than ever.

Many new parents seem to be very good at taking the blame for any perceived shortcomings that their baby displays; yet, they refuse to take credit for the delightful, wonderful things that their baby does. Forget about who gets the credit, or the blame, and enjoy your baby for who he is.

Incidentally, we have no reason to believe that a baby's self-quieting is affected, in any way, by whether his mom works outside the home or whether his mom is married. Self-quieting is a skill with which a baby is born; it's that simple!

Your Baby's General Appearance

Some new parents aren't prepared for how their newborn looks. They may have heard other moms or dads say how pretty new babies look or how babies resemble their mom or their dad. You will be a lot happier if you expect your newborn to look fairly bad. Then, if she looks all right, you will be pleased and if she does not look very good you won't be quite so upset.

Many newborns have discolored skin, some are covered with the products of their delivery, some may have misshaped heads, and some may be wrinkled like a raisin. Some parents of newborns have expressed the sentiment that they wished that someone had warned them about how their babies would look when they were born. You have been warned.

Daily Maintenance

It is very important that you keep your baby in good condition. Daily maintenance involves frequent bathing, hair shampooing, fingernail trimming, cord (belly button) care, and, if necessary, care for a circumcision.

Bathing a Newborn

You should give sponge baths to your new baby until the umbilical cord (belly button) falls off (usually within ten days to three weeks). A sponge bath means that you should not submerge your baby in water. Rather, you should wash your baby with a washcloth or a sponge. You should not get the umbilical cord wet, because this increases the chance that it may become infected.

Before you begin to give your baby a sponge bath, organize all of the materials that you will need. If you're organized, you won't have to interrupt the bath to get any additional items. Spread out a thick bath towel near the bathroom sink or on the kitchen counter and gently place your baby on the towel. Dampen the washcloth or sponge. Begin the bath by washing your baby's face. The water is cleaner at the beginning of the bath and you want the cleanest water possible for cleansing your baby's face. Some parents will wash their baby's face with plain tap water, others will use a very mild soap. After you wash her face, proceed to wash her arms, upper body, legs, and feet. Wash her bottom last. After you have finished bathing her, wrap the towel around her and pick her up.

Most babies will cry during their first few baths; some will cry for the first month or two during all their daily baths. This is very common. Usually their crying only means that they are unsure about what you are doing and that they don't know what's happening to them. Your baby isn't crying because you are doing something wrong with her (with the singular exception of having the water too hot). Nor does she cry because she is scared. If you try to remain calm and go on about the business of washing your baby, you will become more comfortable bathing your baby and your baby will become more comfortable when being bathed. Speak or sing softly to her and act as if there is absolutely nothing to worry about (even if you are shaking on the inside!). As she becomes more accustomed to having a bath, she'll probably enjoy it; she'll particularly enjoy the close contact she'll have with her mom or her dad.

Many babies enjoy their baths a lot. Bath time is a time for the parent and the baby to be close and to interact. Even if your baby cries through most of the bath, you have to pretend that you are comfortable and that you know what you are doing. Some parents are tempted to bathe their baby less frequently because of the crying; they think that the baby is crying because she doesn't like getting a bath. This is a big mistake. If your baby cries or fusses through most of her bath, then you should bathe her more often, not less often. You may need to give her two baths a day until she gets used to being bathed. If you bathe her twice a day, however, skip using soap completely, until you are bathing her only once a day.

If your newborn is circumcised, allow time for the circumcision to heal (usually within ten days to three weeks) before giving him a bath that involves submersion in water. Contact your doctor for instructions on how to clean this area.

Doctors differ in their opinions about how often infants should be bathed. While you are in the hospital, the nurses probably will sponge bathe your newborn once a day. Usually, they also will volunteer to teach you to give your baby a sponge bath. If they do, accept their offer! Schedule the teaching session so the baby's father can be present for the demonstration. If dad doesn't know how to bathe his baby, then he may be reluctant to attempt to bathe her once you are home. Don't settle for watching a videotape of a newborn being bathed. You need hands-on experience. Once you leave the hospital, your baby will be entirely dependent upon you for her baths. The nurses will tell you and Dad to relax. As long as you are careful with your newborn, you should enjoy the time you have to interact with her. Maternity nurses can teach you almost everything that you need to know about bathing a new baby; they have bathed so many babies that they are very relaxed when giving a bath. The nurses will probably also tell you not to bathe your baby in the bathtub until she's much older, unless you have a sponge insert for the bathtub that supports the baby and keeps her from rolling over during the bath.

Bathing an Infant

When the umbilical cord and circumcision have healed, you can begin bathing your baby in a baby tub or on a sponge insert for the bathtub or sink. Using the sink is usually easier because it does not involve as much bending over as using a bathtub does. Wash your baby's face before putting him in the water. This helps prevent bacteria from getting onto his face during the bath. Then, with a washcloth, wash his arms and legs. Always wash his bottom last. If you are going to trim his fingernails or toenails, let him soak in the water long enough to soften his nails; softer nails are easier to trim.

It is important that your hot water heater is set at 120 degrees. If it is set at a higher temperature, you easily can burn or scald your baby. If the water temperature measures 150 degrees, your baby can get a full-thickness or third-degree burn in only two seconds. When the water temperature measures at 120 degrees, your baby would have to be in the water for ten minutes before he would get a full-thickness burn. Sometimes your baby may be fussy and hard-to-handle during his bath. He may kick his arms and legs and kick off the cold water accidentally. If that happens, only hot water would be pouring from the faucet. If your hot water heater is set at 120 degrees, you have given yourself valuable time to react before your baby is scalded. The chart shows how much time elapses before your baby gets burned.

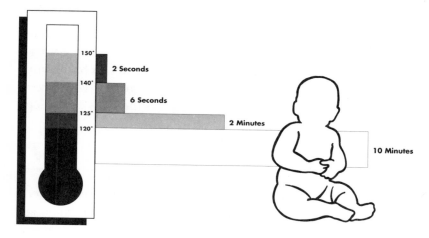

You may think that your dishes or clothes will not get quite as clean if your hot water heater is set at 120 degrees or less. However, detergent manufacturers have developed soap to work best between 120 and 125 degrees. Because less energy is needed to heat water at 120 degrees than to heat water at 145 degrees, you may notice that you save money on your utility bills. One disadvantage to lowering your hot water heater setting is that you may have to be a little more careful when you take your bath, because you may run out of hot water a little sooner. Adults will get burned by water above 130 degrees; that's why the bathtub has both hot and cold water faucets—so you can adjust the temperature. However, with an infant, don't take the chance.

Children should not be left unattended in the bathtub before their fourth birthday. The temptation to leave them alone for a minute is great as they get a little older, but the price you would pay if your baby had an accident is too great. Wouldn't you feel like a complete idiot if your baby got hurt in the bathtub while you were answering a phone call from somebody selling magazine subscriptions? Get into the habit of ignoring the telephone if you are in the middle of any important child-care situation.

Because you will be bathing your baby for at least four years, you might as well start doing things to make bath time more enjoyable. You can talk or sing to your baby throughout the bath. If you don't know any "bathing" songs, then make one up. Babies aren't critical. They enjoy almost any kind of singing. As you get more comfortable and more confident at

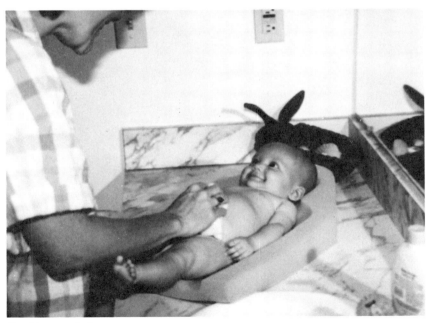

Bathing an infant

bath time, you'll find that your baby stays calmer. Bath time is a good time to check your baby, from head to toe. You can stimulate his skin with the washcloth as you are bathing him by rubbing it across his arms and legs and up and down his chest and back. He also will be stimulated by the changes in the air temperature of the room to the temperature of the water, then back to the room temperature. Don't become unduly concerned about your baby getting chilled. Most of the time the room temperature in the bathroom is almost the same as the temperature in the rest of the house.

Hair Shampooing

If your new baby doesn't cry during her bath, she's almost certain to cry the first few times that you shampoo her hair. The

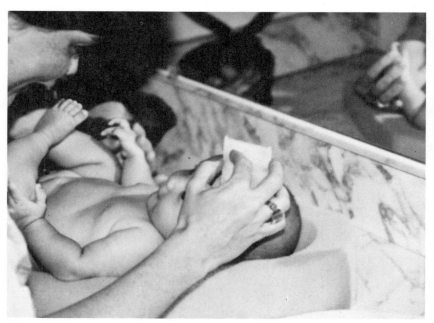

Shampooing the baby's hair

same procedures should be applied to shampooing that are applied to bathing. That is, be calm and matter-of-fact; speak softly to your baby all of the time (even if she's screaming the entire time) and pretend that you know what you are doing. The more she cries during the hair shampooing, the more often you should shampoo her hair. She'll quickly learn what's going on and quit being fussy. If you wash her hair once or twice a day, don't use soap or shampoo; instead, use tap water. That way you can get your baby accustomed to having her hair washed without worrying about irritation to her scalp. As soon as she's used to having her hair washed, you will need to wash it only about twice a week. If you observe an unusual condition such as redness, rash, or flaking, then you should contact her physician.

You may find that your baby's hair is easier to wash if you wrap her in a towel or blanket first. This provides her with a feeling of security and gives you a much better grip on her. After she's wrapped, you can hold her on your hip, similar to the way a football player carries a football, with her head slightly raised toward the sink. Use a soft-bristle brush to remove any food or dirt from her scalp. Read the labels on all products that you use on your baby, including hair shampoo. Any product that states it should be kept away from children is probably best kept away from babies. Buy only gentle, baby shampoo that does not have perfumes or additives like deodorants; additives are generally unnecessary for cleansing purposes and your baby may have a reaction to one of them. Even though a product may state on the label that it is safe for baby's skin, if it gets into your baby's eyes, you can count on her crying.

Fingernail Trimming

Your baby's nails must be kept short to keep them from scratching his face while he innocently is moving his hands. Some babies actually are born with fingernails that are long

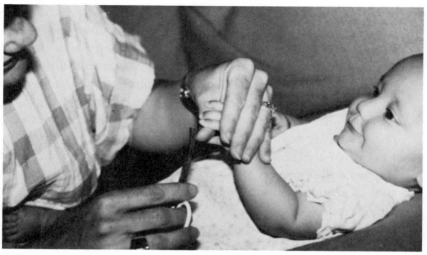

Trimming the baby's nails

enough to be trimmed while they are still in the hospital. If you have any question about whether they need to be trimmed, ask your nurse. If your baby's nails need trimming, ask for a demonstration and ask to trim a couple of nails so that you can learn how to do it correctly before you take her home. Hospital nurses usually recommend that you use small, rounded-end infant nail scissors. The small, pocket fingernail clippers that you squeeze to effect the cutting (like the ones manufactured by Trim™) work well because they are easier to control and you don't have to worry about sticking your baby.

Parents may find that the best time for trimming nails is either after a bath, during a feeding, or while their baby is asleep, because these are times when their baby is most content and happy. At first it may be a two-person job, with one person feeding the baby and the other trimming the nails. With your hand covering your baby's hand, gently expose one finger at a time and trim towards your hand. This allows you to maintain firm control so that your baby can't jerk away and cause you to nip his finger.

Belly Button

No matter how your baby was born, he will start out with a clamp on his belly button. The clamp is placed on the umbilical cord about an inch or so away from the belly immediately after delivery and removed before you leave the delivery room. Within ten days to three weeks, the umbilical cord will dry up and fall off, leaving behind what will later look like a regular belly button. Before the cord dries up and falls off, you need to swab the cord and the area around the cord gently with a piece of cotton soaked in alcohol. The alcohol helps keep the area clean and speeds up the drying process. It's a good idea to diaper your baby in such a way so that the diaper does not rub directly against the cord. You can fold down the front of the diaper before pinning or taping the sides together. Some mothers pin the baby's shirt up to keep it off of the cord.

If the area around the cord becomes infected (which is unusual, but not serious), contact the baby's doctor for advice. You can tell that the area is infected if the belly button or the cord has a foul-smelling drainage or if the area is warmer to your

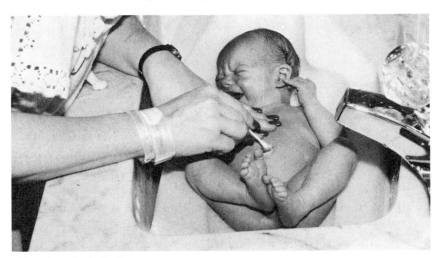

Cleaning the belly button

touch than the rest of the baby. A lot of new parents aren't prepared for just how grundgy a normal umbilical cords gets, so be prepared for an ugly, black, yucky cord.

Circumcision

If you decide to have your baby circumcised, the circumcision usually is done during the second or third day of life. Some religions specify that the procedure be performed seven days

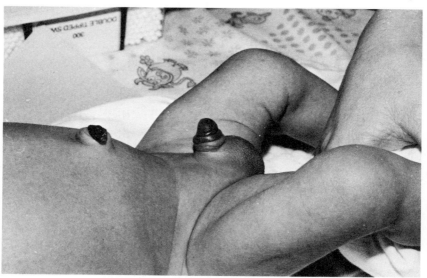

A circumcised baby

after birth as part of a religious ceremony. The American Academy of Pediatrics, with the support of the American College of Obstetrics and Gynecology, has taken the position that circumcision should be an elective procedure, done only after the baby's parents are informed about the advantages and disadvantages of circumcision and allowed to decide if they want their baby circumcised. Although doctors used to tell parents that circumcision was a painless procedure, recent research indicates that it is painful.

There are several different ways to circumcise a baby; the procedure used is determined by the doctor's preference. If you have trouble deciding whether to have your baby circumcised, consider talking to a urologist (a doctor who specializes in the diagnosis and treatment of disorders of the urinary tract). Whether you decide to have your baby circumcised or not, ask your baby's doctor for specific instructions on how to take care of your baby's penis.

Diaper Changes

Few parents, with their first baby, are prepared for the number of diaper changes their baby needs. The average newborn goes through about one hundred diapers a week—that's right—one hundred diapers a week. The good thing about having this many diaper changes in one week is that you quickly become an expert on diapering. Because new babies cry a lot, be prepared for some crying the first couple of weeks when you change your baby's diaper. The best training you can get is to make sure that both Mom and Dad have been shown how to change a diaper under a nurse's supervision before leaving the hospital. This practice should be with your baby, not with a doll. After all, you're taking your baby home from the hospital with you, not a doll.

With one hundred diaper changes a week, you need to be careful not to do anything to make your baby's bottom sore. Carefully clean the area with something like a dampened washcloth or a commercially available premoistened towelette (for example, Dab-a-Ways™, Wet-Ones™). There's no need to rub hard or go back and forth over the area too many times; just clean the bottom and let it dry before putting on a fresh diaper. With a baby boy, the bowel movement or urine may get into the grooves in his scrotum (the sack that holds the testicles) and with a baby girl, it may find its way into the outer folds of her vagina (actually the outer lips or the labia). With a baby girl, doctors recommend that you always clean from the front to the back, making only one sweeping motion with each clean cloth or moist towelette. This way you are less likely to move the BM into the vagina or the urethra (the opening for urine). Fecal material left in this area is the main cause of urinary tract infections in infants.

Many products are marketed to use after a diaper change, but, generally, all you need to do is clean the baby's bottom, give it a chance to dry, and put on a fresh diaper. Some parents try to speed up the drying by waving their hands, or the fresh diaper, back and forth to direct air across the baby's bottom. If you have a hand-held hair dryer that has a cool setting, you might want to use it to dry your baby's bottom, particularly if he is bothered by diaper rash. Unless his doctor or nurse specifically tells you to use something on his bottom, it is better to use nothing on it. Many products, such as petroleum jelly, cornstarch, and baby powder, contribute to diaper rash by clogging the skin pores.

When you change your baby's diaper, try talking or singing to him softly. He will become accustomed to the sound of your voice and reach the point where he won't cry during diaper changes. You can describe to him what you are doing, while you are doing it. Don't worry that people around you may think that you have lost your mind; your baby may learn to really like it.

Some people have the notion that they are the only people who know how to put on a diaper correctly. For example, some parents think that the tapes that fasten a disposable diaper must always stick towards the back of the diaper. If Mom is the person who usually changes the baby's diaper and she sees Dad put on a fresh diaper with the tapes sticking towards the front, she may get a big laugh out of it, unfortunately at Dad's expense. Although this may seem like a really small thing, it can discourage Dad from wanting to help with the baby. As long as Dad puts on the diaper so that it stays on, there should be no concern

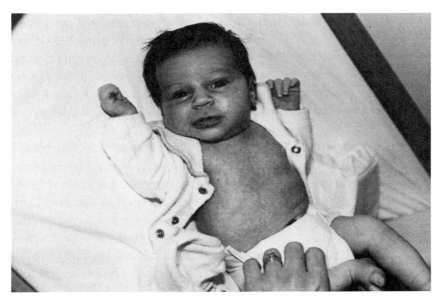

Changing the baby's diaper

whether it's on frontward or backward. In fact, if the manufacturers of disposable diapers thought there were a front and a back, they would have marked the diapers accordingly. Be thankful that someone is giving you a helping hand and try not to be critical.

The same point can be made with other caregiving tasks. There is no right way to put on baby buntings or to wrap babies in blankets. If you are critical of how other caregivers perform routine tasks for your baby, you may discourage them from helping with your baby in the future. Unless what you see is absolutely intolerable or puts the baby in jeopardy, be thankful that someone cares enough to help you.

Skin Care

With the exception of diaper changes, your baby usually will not need any special care for her skin. Routine bathing with a mild baby soap is all that is necessary. Remember, though, to dry your baby gently, especially those little fat creases around her knees and elbows. Babies do not need to be coated with baby oil, powders, or lotions. They only need to be gently cleaned and carefully dried off. Using a lotion could cause a rash or may disguise a rash and make the healing process take longer.

Babies under one year of age need protection to prevent them from getting sunburned. Their skin is very tender and can get sunburned easily. All babies, regardless of their race, can get sunburned. If you want to spend time in the sun, keep your baby shaded from the sun and apply a sunscreen to exposed skin. On cloudy, overcast days, your baby still needs protection. If your baby is outside for very long, be sure that all skin is covered with lightweight clothing or a good sunscreen or both.

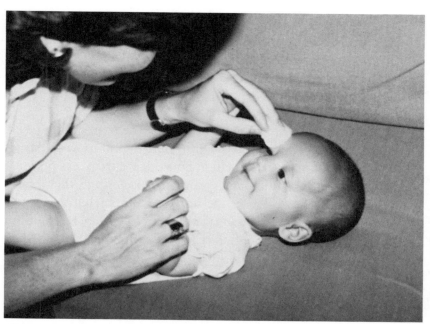

Cleaning the baby's eyes

Eyes

Your baby's eyes can be checked and cleaned during the daily bath. More frequent checking is usually unnecessary. When bathing your baby, wet a cotton ball, squeeze most of the water out, and then gently wipe, from the edge of the eyelid nearest the nose to the outside edge, across the eyelid once or twice. Nothing should be put into your baby's eyes without the specific advice of the baby's doctor. Never use over-the-counter medications in your baby's eyes unless specifically instructed to do so by a physician. The tears in the baby's eyes are sufficient to cleanse the underside of the eyelid and the eyeball itself.

Ears

Your baby's outer ear lobes can be cleaned easily, during his bath, with a damp washcloth or a wet cotton ball. Resist the temptation to clean your baby's ear canal with any instrument such as a cotton swab.

Do not try to clean out any build-up of ear wax yourself. The ear drum is only a short distance inside the ear canal and any attempt to probe inside the ear risks injury or permanent damage to your baby's eardrum. If ear wax becomes a problem, your baby's doctor or nurse will clean the ear with a special instrument or will tell you to obtain a solution from your druggist that will gently dissolve the ear wax. You will notice that your doctor always checks your baby's ears during regular office visits. If there is too much wax build-up, it will be attended to at that time.

Nose

Most hospitals will provide you with a small rubber bulb that can be used for cleaning out your baby's nose and mouth. Before you leave the hospital, ask one of the maternity nurses to show you how to suction your baby's nose and mouth. This is a very simple process. Squeeze the bulb, insert the tip of the syringe (the long narrow end) into your baby's nose or the back of his mouth, and release the pressure on the bulb. When released, this creates a vacuum that will draw the nasal secretions into the bulb. Remember to clean the bulb so it is ready to use the next time you need it. To clean it, simply squeeze and release the bulb several times with the tip in clean water. This will

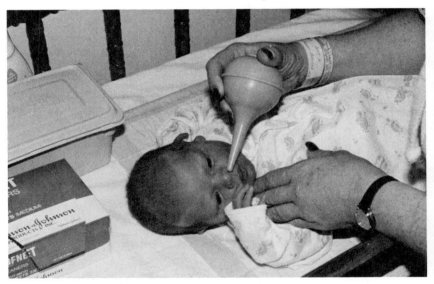

Suctioning the baby's nose

force out whatever was sucked into it. Be sure it is empty and dry before the next use. You will notice that your baby doesn't like to be suctioned. This is typical and really quite reasonable—nobody wants to have a rubber bulb stuck up his nose! However, you will also notice that babies do not know how to blow their noses, particularly when you ask them to, so they really don't have much choice. When you do have to clean out his nose, do it firmly, but quickly.

It is a good idea to keep the bulb near your baby when you are feeding (either breast or bottle), burping, or changing a diaper. You don't want to have to look all over the place to find the bulb if your baby's nose or mouth needs suctioned.

Clothing

A little common sense is necessary when choosing clothing for your baby. Babies are comfortable in a wide range of temperatures. If the temperature is eighty degrees, your baby doesn't need more than a diaper, as long as he is protected from the sun's rays. Conversely, your baby needs to be kept warm when the temperature is cool. However, some of the old notions about keeping a baby bundled up, even in the summer, are not true. As the layering of several thin garments in cool weather is a good idea with adults, it is a good idea for your baby, too. When you and your baby go indoors, you can remove some of the layers of clothing and when you go outdoors, you can add layers. This is true particularly when your baby is wearing a heavy snowsuit; you don't want your baby to be cold inside when you take off his snowsuit, so be sure he is wearing several layers of clothing. A good guideline to use is that your baby will be comfortable dressed in the same type of clothing in which you are dressed.

Other considerations should be made when choosing clothing for your baby. First, if your baby's skin is irritated by a particular fiber or material, then avoid clothing containing that material. Second, don't dress your baby in an outfit that has strings on the outside, including pretty little waistbands. These can become wrapped around your baby and cause discomfort or could cause choking or strangulation. Third, because you know you are going to have to be changing diapers, choose outfits that will allow you to change them easily.

The Trip Home

Most new parents think that it's both exciting to take their new baby home from the hospital and a little bit scary because they will be on their own with the new baby for the first time. They never dreamed that the trip would involve as many details as it does. To begin with, you first have to decide what you and your baby need for the trip home from the hospital. Someone should bring an outfit for the baby to wear, a receiving blanket (that's a fancy word for a tiny, thin blanket that you can wrap the baby in), and additional blankets or clothing, depending on the weather. Try to keep in mind that whatever is brought to the hospital has to go home. In fact, it's a good idea for someone to start taking home the gifts, plants, candy, and other belongings that you have accumulated during your hospital stay a day before your expected discharge date. Why? Because there's only so much junk that you can fit into one car or truck!

Hospital Discharge

Because Mom and baby are doing fine doesn't mean that you are free to leave the hospital. Both Mom and baby have to get their discharge papers first. If Mom was admitted to the hospital by her obstetrician, then the obstetrician must write out and sign her discharge orders; without these, she can't leave the hospital. If the baby has a different doctor, then the baby's doctor has to write and sign the nursery discharge orders for the baby. When you have both sets of discharge orders ready, then Mom or Dad is ready to go to the hospital business office to complete the paperwork, which includes arranging for payment of the hospital bill. At some time during this process, a nurse or an aide may offer you the option of renting a child passenger safety seat (which might be called a safety seat, an infant restraint seat, or a car seat). If you don't already have a safety seat, then rent one. A safety seat provides you with a safe, convenient way to travel in an automobile with your baby. Babies who travel in an auto safety seat are more comfortable because they travel securely—they aren't sliding around on the seat of the car. You don't have to worry about them falling over if you go around a corner or pitching forward if you stop suddenly. Babies also sleep better in a safety seat. You can carry your baby to and from the car in a safety seat or use it in your home as a feeding chair or as a way to prop up your baby when she's awake and alert but tired of lying on her stomach.

The Trip Home

Some parents think that the best way to travel in a car with a baby is to carry the baby in their arms, where they can hold and protect him. Unfortunately, nothing is further from the truth. In fact, the most dangerous place in the car for your baby is in an adult passenger's arms or lap. Why? Because, in the event that the driver makes a sudden maneuver, such as turning quickly or braking hard, or if the vehicle were involved in an accident, not only would your baby be thrown forward or to the side, but the adult who was holding the baby would also fly in exactly the same direction and could crush or injure the baby in the process.

Probably the biggest mistake that parents make concerning infant safety seats is in thinking that a flimsy, plastic feeding chair is safe for use in the automobile. Not only does a feeding chair not protect an infant while in the car, its usage lures you into a false sense of security that your baby is safe and that you don't need to get one of those expensive infant car seats. When you plan for the furniture that you need for your new baby, you have to plan for an infant car seat along with the crib and the changing table.

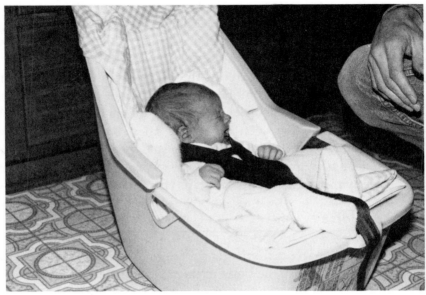

An infant safety seat

Another important consideration is that the law in all fifty states requires you to restrain your baby in a federally approved infant restraint seat every time your baby travels in a car. It is illegal and unsafe to have a baby in your arms, in a feeding chair, or in a travel bed when you are in the car. Transporting an unrestrained infant or a young child by automobile is, without question, the most dangerous thing you do.

Why don't some parents use safety seats in the car? In the past, parents did not know about the benefits of safety seats, but that's no longer true. Now, parents don't use safety seats because they don't like the nuisance of maneuvering their baby in and out of the safety seat every time they travel in a car, whether on short trips in town or on longer trips. Some older safety seats have special straps on top (called tether straps) that must be fastened to a seat belt when the safety seat is used in the front seat or to the car's chassis when it is used in the back seat. The tether strap is rather inconvenient and even annoying, but it's certainly better to use the tether strap than to risk injury to your baby.

Some people won't restrain their baby in a safety seat because they are afraid that they won't be able to unfasten their baby from the seat fast enough if their car were to catch on fire or to sink in a river or lake. Fortunately, very few cars (less than one percent) catch on fire or end up under water. Your baby is always safer in a restraint seat.

In addition to the safety aspects of using a safety seat, five additional reasons also should be considered. First, when your baby gets older, you will find that she behaves better in the car if she's riding in a safety seat. She will be less likely to stick her head out the windows, climb from the front seat to the back, or turn up the radio suddenly. When two children are in the car, you will find that it is harder, though not impossible, for them to fight with each other if they are secured in their safety seats.

Second, toddlers and older children are less likely to experience car sickness or motion sickness if they ride in a safety seat because they can look at the scenery rather than looking only at the objects inside the car. The closer an object is, the more the eyes move to stay focused on it. The rapid eye movements that are necessary to keep close things (such as objects inside the car) in focus contribute to car sickness. Children are less prone to get sick when they sit high enough so that they can look out the car window and see the scenery. By sitting in a safety seat, children can sit high enough. The same effect will help counter the feeling of seasickness. If children sit on the deck of the boat where they can look at things in the distance, they will feel less sick than if they if they sit below deck.

Third, toddlers as well as infants sleep better in the comfort and security of a safety seat. Children alternate periods of dozing off, looking around, chattering or singing, or playing with their toys.

Fourth, infants and children are less likely to distract the driver if they are in a safety seat. In fact, when children are passengers in cars, forty-two percent of accidents are either caused by or attributed to the driver being distracted by a child.

Fifth, your infant or toddler is less likely to get hurt inside the car. Children can fall off the seat or fall out the window. In the United States, about forty children are killed each year by falling out the window or door of a car. No child properly fastened in a safety seat has ever fallen out of a car.

When you travel with your infant in the car, you should follow a few simple rules.

1. If both parents are traveling in the car, one adult and the baby should ride in the back seat. The baby should be in an infant safety seat which is connected to the car with the seat belt so that the baby rides facing backward.

2. If only one parent is traveling with the baby, the baby should ride in the front passenger seat and be correctly restrained. Some safety experts recommend that an infant always be restrained in the back seat. Unfortunately, when your infant is in the back seat, you cannot see her and you may become very anxious. You may be turning around a lot to see your baby and not paying attention to driving. You can interact more easily with your baby if she is restrained in the front seat. However, if you feel comfortable with your baby restrained in the back seat, you should travel that way.

3. A safety seat is the most comfortable place for your baby to sleep and you don't have to worry about her safety. Any time that your baby is asleep in the car, don't disturb her; leave her alone.

4. When your baby is awake and behaving nicely, either by being quiet and looking around or by jabbering, be sure that you interact with her periodically. In this way, your baby will

learn to enjoy automobile travel because you are fun to ride with. You can touch her, sing or hum songs, talk about what you are doing or where you are going (for example, "We're going to see Nana and Papa."). If your baby has a favorite blanket, place it next to or in the safety seat within her reach.

5. Carry one or two stuffed toys that your baby will learn to associate with quiet travel. A good idea is to have special, quiet toys that are played with only in the car. These toys help to decrease boredom. Remember, your baby's attention span is very short. Don't expect her to keep herself occupied for more than a couple of minutes at a time.

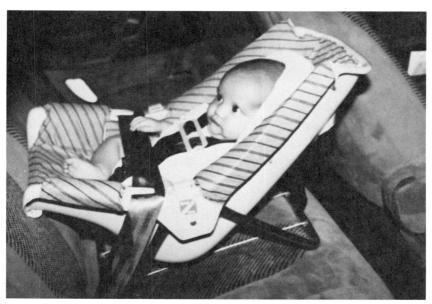

Secured for the ride

6. Ignore yelling, screaming, and begging. The instant that your baby is quiet, begin touching her or talking or singing to her. Do not yell, scream, or nag at your baby. Never take your baby out of her safety seat while the car is moving to hold her. To do so will teach her that if she cries, you will take her out

of her safety seat. If your baby is crying and it is time for a feeding, pull off the road and stop to feed her. Some people are reluctant to stop periodically, because they're usually in a big hurry to get wherever they're going. Some parents will use any excuse—feedings, diaper changes, burping—to take their baby out of the safety seat. Remember, if you transport your baby without the benefit of a safety seat, you're not fooling anyone; you're risking your baby's life.

7. Older brothers and sisters should behave in the car and ride with their seat belts on or in a safety seat. Children who grow up routinely using a safety seat or seat belt feel as natural wearing a seat belt when they are older as their parents feel traveling without one.

8. With your frequent praise, touching, and attention, your baby will remain interested and busy with her surroundings. If you pay some attention to her, she will not spend her time crying.

9. Many parents like to rest their right arm near the front edge of the safety seat so that they can hold the baby's hand, rearrange her clothing, or just play with her. Babies like this kind of attention and will ride better in the car if you do this some of the time.

10. If your baby is traveling in an automobile with other people, such as grandparents or baby-sitters, insist that they transport your baby correctly restrained in her safety seat. Often you see children riding on the folded-down arm rest in the front seat of the car. You would not endanger your baby's life in any other way, so don't be foolish enough to let anyone ride with your baby on a launching platform to certain disaster.

11. When you baby is around nine to twelve months of age, you will need to either switch to a toddler safety seat (if you've been using an infant safety seat) or to change the riding position of the safety seat (if it is the convertible type). If the instructions on your infant seat are gone or hard to understand, ask your infant's pediatrician or nurse when to switch to a toddler safety

seat. Your child should use a safety seat until she is about eight to ten years old, when she can comfortably see out of the car with only a seat belt on, and when the seat belt fits correctly across the bones of her pelvis.

12. Be sure to wear your own seat belt, even if you are pregnant. Babies don't make good orphans. Now that more and more parents are using safety seats for their children, there has been an increase in the number of accidents in which the babies in safety seats were not injured, but the parents were either injured or killed, because they were not wearing seat belts. Please take good care or your baby's only Mommy and Daddy.

13. If you must transport a young child in an automobile and you cannot use a safety seat, the seat belt will provide some protection. Make sure that your child is sitting up, with the seat belt placed low around her pelvis.

If you really want your baby to enjoy traveling in the car and you want your baby to be as safe as possible, you have one and only one choice—use an approved safety seat every time you take your baby in the car.

Preparation of the Baby's Room

Many expectant parents enjoy decorating the baby's room during the last month or two before their baby is born. They can choose colors for the walls, choose furnishings, and decorate at their leisure. Some of the more obvious areas to consider include the baby's bed, the changing area, the bathing area, and some provision for the baby when she's awake and just watching what's going on around her.

The Crib

If you haven't noticed already, a baby crib can be very expensive. When shopping for the crib or when considering accepting a generous offer for the loan of a crib, there are six features that must be considered. First, the crib bars must be no more than 2³/₈ inches apart. The bars must be spaced this closely so your baby cannot get her head caught between the crib bars. Do not rely on a bumper pad for this protection. A bumper pad is padding that rests on the four sides of the mattress and extends up about eight to ten inches. The bumper pad can protect your baby's head from banging into the bars, but do not rely on the pad to keep her head from getting caught between the bars.

Second, look for a crib that has a double safety latch on the side rails. Before the side can be lowered, the double safety latch must be released by pressing it with your foot. This is a very

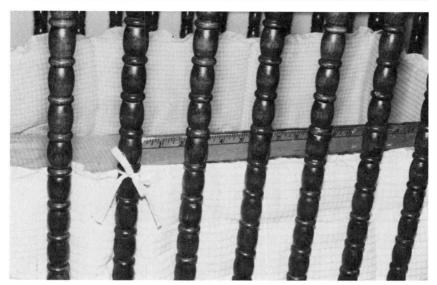

Above: Crib bars are 2⅜ inches apart

Below: Crib safety latch

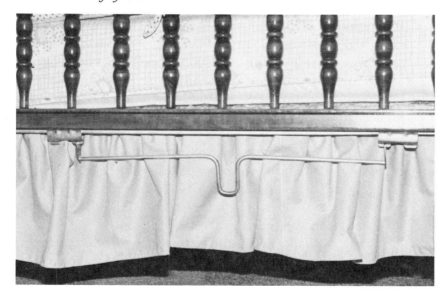

Babies enjoy mobiles over their cribs

handy feature since you'll usually have both hands on the baby
when you're either picking her up or placing her back into her
crib. Many cribs also have a good safety feature to guard
against the side rails falling down. The side rails must be lifted
slightly while pressing the foot latch, in order to lower the side.
The purpose of this lift feature is for the protection of your baby.
If you don't have this lift-first feature, then when your baby is
older and able to crawl she could hit the foot latch with her head
and cause the side railing to fall on the back of her head or neck.

Third, the crib mattress should be no less than twenty-two
inches from the top of the side rails, when they both are in their
highest position. This will help to guard your baby against
falls.

Fourth, check the crib itself to ensure that there are no
decorations containing either small balls that might come loose
and get stuck in your baby's throat, or rattles that contain small
pellets or balls that could be inhaled or swallowed by your baby
if the rattles should break.

Fifth, with older cribs, be certain that the paint on the crib
is not lead based. If babies find any chipped paint, either on the
crib or anywhere else in the house, they are very likely to put

some of the paint chips in their mouth, which would result in serious medical problems. If you have even the slightest suspicion that there is lead-paint in an area that is accessible to your baby, the lead paint must be removed. Don't make the mistake of painting over the lead paint to protect your baby. The lead paint hazard will be just as great when the new paint peels or chips.

Sixth, try to provide a mobile or other stimulating crib toys for your baby. As babies get a little older, they enjoy having some kind of mobile hanging over their crib. They will spend long periods of time pushing the parts of the mobile or just watching the parts move around. Some mobiles also have a music box. Some babies love the music box, some don't seem to notice it, and some don't like it.

The Changing Area

It is a good idea to have a special changing area that is big enough to hold all of the stuff you need when you change your

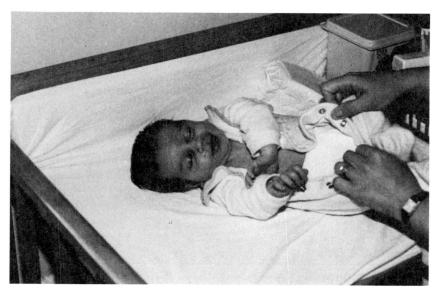

The changing area

baby's diaper; try to make the changing area high enough to reduce the strain on your back, because you will be changing a lot of diapers during the first six months. You can even put a small changing pad on top of your baby's dresser if it is the right height to make changing comfortable. The changing supplies can be stored between the changing pad and the wall behind the dresser.

It is very important to remember to keep the baby powder out of your baby's reach, so he cannot pick it up and play with the container. If he squeezes the container, he can get the powder on his face. He could then inhale the fine powder, which could result in severe respiratory problems. If your baby should inhale some powder, contact a physician immediately for emergency treatment.

The baby's closet

The Baby's Closet

Because babies clothes are so little, you will have a lot of wasted space in the closet when their clothes are hung up. Their little outfits only reach down about one foot from the clothes-hanger rod, thus leaving a big empty space between the bottom of the clothes and the junk that you have piled on the floor. Several manufacturers of juvenile furniture offer a clever device that hooks over the regular clothes pole and extends down to a second pole which is about halfway between the existing pole and the floor. This provides you with an additional 2 $\frac{1}{2}$ feet of closet space. Later, when your child is older and you want to begin teaching him to hang up his clothes, having the lower pole changes an otherwise impossible task into a simple one.

Common Operating Characteristics

Every year new parents are faced with the challenge of discovering how their newborn functions from day to day. New parents usually don't have a lot of information on what to expect from their baby, except for what they have read from a book or what they have imagined in their mind. Babies sleep, cry, and eat. This chapter helps you understand and enjoy their daily patterns.

Sleeping

The average newborn sleeps about sixteen to twenty hours each day. The remaining hours are spent nursing and in standard caregiving such as diapering, dressing, and bathing. At first, your baby will be sleeping around the clock, with your caregiving interspersed at six roughly equal times. As your baby grows older and matures, he will be awake for increasingly longer periods of time.

Many new parents get concerned when they listen to their baby sleep, because babies don't sleep like adults do. They often make noises, gurgling sounds, or sighs. They also may have fitful sleep, appearing to the new parent as though they are not sleeping comfortably. If your baby's sleep bothers you, then either watch him sleeping often enough so that you get used to it, or don't watch him sleeping at all. Many anxious parents look for any kind of excuse to pick up their baby; if you keep disturbing your baby by picking him up, you will deny him the opportunity to get some much needed rest. Use a little common sense. If someone came into your room every five to ten minutes to see if you were all right, you'd probably have a hard time getting any sleep! Most adults cannot go to sleep the instant their heads hit the pillow. When adults are awakened in the middle of the night, after having had several hours of good sound sleep, they can have trouble going back to sleep. Try turning the situation around. Parents cannot expect their baby to go to sleep almost instantly. Try to remember that your baby has no way of telling you that he is tired and wants to rest. The only way he can communicate this to you is by crying. Yet, when he cries, your instinct is to go into his room and pick him up.

If you have doubts about why your baby is crying, rule out all of the normal concerns such as a dirty diaper, gas, or hunger, and then put him to bed and leave him completely alone for at least ten to fifteen minutes. If you have to check on him, keep the light off, don't pick him up, and don't talk to him. Just pat him once or twice and leave his room. If he is tired and you haven't been interrupting his sleep during the previous weeks, he will probably surprise you and go to sleep. Although it is hard for many parents to understand, babies need to learn good sleep habits as much as they need to learn other important skills. If you begin a reasonable approach to sleep, your baby will be more likely to develop good, sound sleep habits.

To put things into perspective, think about the everyday things that your baby can't do—he can't talk, he can't go for a walk, and he can't get himself a drink. However, one of the few things that every baby knows how to do well is cry, and babies will cry. But because your baby cries when you put him to bed or cries when he wakes up in the morning doesn't mean he is unhappy, distressed, abandoned, or unloved; he's just doing the one thing that he knows how to do well. Look at the reasons for his crying from another perspective; your baby is not capable of thinking in the abstract terms of missing something or someone. He is not lying in his bed thinking to himself that "if my parents really loved me, they'd come in here and pick me up." As an infant, he is not capable of thinking in such abstractions.

If you are concerned about your baby not getting enough sleep, the first thing to check is your habits. How much are you bugging your baby? Are you leaving him alone long enough to fall asleep before you go in to check on him? Usually, the reason that parents charge into their baby's room at the first sound of crying has little to do with their baby. The problem is that they have little patience with the crying. They're not worried about their baby's psyche, they're worried about their own. Babies who go to bed with the least trouble are the same babies who sleep soundly and who sleep the longest. Babies who go to bed at 11:00 P.M. and wake up at 5:00 A.M., in addition to waking up one or two times each night have the most bedtime and nighttime problems later on.

Two practices that you should consider if you are experiencing bedtime problems with your baby are closing the baby's bedroom door at night and turning off the night-light in the baby's room when you're out of the room. Fire-safety experts recommend that bedroom doors be kept closed at night. If a fire should break out in the house, there will be less air available to feed the fire if all the interior doors are shut. You still will be able to hear your baby through the closed door if he gets sick during the night. In fact, parents rarely sleep on those nights when their baby is sick even with something as common as an ear infection.

The only two reasons for a baby to have a night-light burning are if he likes to read for relaxation before retiring or if he is entertaining friends in his room at bedtime. The night-light is for Mom and Dad, not for the baby. Your baby didn't have a night-light in the womb nor was the door open, yet somehow he made it through without any apparent ill effects.

When putting your child to bed, you should put him to bed in the same place where you expect him to wake up. You may wake up every morning and find your child sleeping in your bed. If you feel that you cannot prevent this from happening or if you simply don't want to do anything about it, then you should put him to bed in your bed. Doing so will save him a trip through the house, in the dark, in the middle of the night, going from his bed to yours. If you don't want to put him to bed in your bed or have him wake up in your bed, then don't allow this habit to start.

Crying

Newborn babies average about one-and-one-half to two hours of crying each day. Fortunately their crying usually occurs throughout the day at numerous times rather than at one stretch. Throughout the first five to six weeks of life, the amount of time that your baby cries increases. When your baby is six weeks old, she is crying almost three hours each day. The average baby cries more at six weeks of age than she did at one week of age, no matter what the parents do! Some mothers who decide to breast-feed their baby feel concerned because their baby cries more the third week than the second week; often they will wonder if the crying is "their fault." Nothing is further from the truth. The increase in crying over the first month to six weeks is normal and healthy.

Fortunately, from about six weeks to twelve weeks, the amount of crying decreases no matter what the parents do! By about three months of age, the average baby is down to about one hour of crying each day. That one hour seems to hold constant for at least the first year. As children get older, they don't cry less often, but they cry for different reasons.

Most parents find that their babies cry more during the evening hours than at any other time; most babies cry more often between 7:00 P.M. and 10:00 P.M. than they do at any other time. If your baby's daytime caregiver reports that your baby rarely cries during the day and you think that your baby cries a lot throughout the evening, don't be concerned. It is very common for babies to fuss more in the evening than at any other time. Professionals don't really know why this is so.

You can do two things to decrease the amount of crying your baby does. One time when you can really have an effect on the amount of crying your baby does is when she begins to awaken after a nap or after a night's sleep. During your baby's

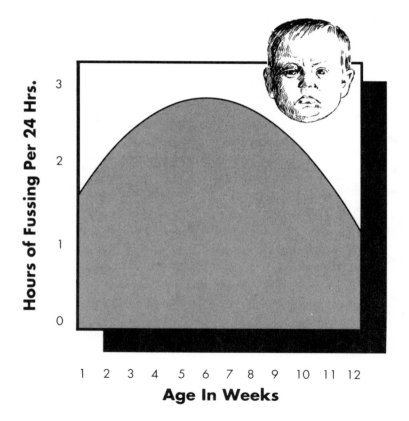

first two or three months of life, she can go from a sound sleep to a full blown cry in an instant. However, after she is two or three months old, she will wake up and make cute noises before she starts crying. If you go into her room and pick her up while she is still making her cute little noises, she'll be very pleasant in the morning and you will have figured out one way to reduce the total amount of crying in a day. Over time, she'll learn to lie in her crib and make cute little noises, knowing that you will be in in a minute to pick her up, change her diaper, and feed her. If, on the other hand, you wait until the cute little noises stop and she starts to cry, then she is learning that the only way to get you to pick her up is to cry. It's your choice. You can start the day with crying or with cute little noises. Make your choice.

There's an interesting phenomenon that is commonly seen in many households. When the baby awakens in the morning, both parents lie very still, hoping the other one will get up to get the baby. While the parents are "playing possum," the baby gives up and starts crying. A better way to handle the morning would be to agree, the night before, who will get up with the baby. Then, the one who agrees to get up will do so right away and let the other one get some rest.

The second way to decrease the amount of crying that your baby does is by developing good bedtime habits for your baby. Parents who put their baby to bed in a matter-of-fact manner and leave her alone will find that she will learn that her bed is a place where she goes to sleep. Over time, when she is put to bed she will go to sleep more easily.

Most parents never dreamed that their baby would tear at their heart strings so strongly. No parent enjoys listening to the baby cry. No parent can sit in the living room and smile, knowing that the baby is in her room crying her heart out. If you don't enjoy hearing your baby cry, then resolve from the beginning to do nothing that will contribute unnecessarily to her crying. When you can put her to bed and let her cry for a couple of minutes, you do it not because you enjoy hearing her cry, but because you know that you have to do that in order to establish good bedtime habits.

Having your baby fall asleep in your arms is cute when the baby is a week or two old, but it loses its cuteness by the time the baby is a year-and-a-half old. Everybody has to learn how to go to bed, relax, and fall asleep at some time in their life. The younger a person is when this is learned, the easier it is to learn it. If you don't let your child learn this until he is three or four years old, it will take a great deal of patience and perseverance to fix it, and it will be hard on both parent and child.

All babies must learn how to make the transition from being awake to being asleep. After your baby is three months old, if he routinely falls asleep while he is being breast-fed, then he learns to use the breast as a transition object. If he goes to sleep for his naps in addition to the night while breast-feeding, then he also will need to be breast-fed to fall asleep if he awakens in the middle of the night. The same phenomenon is true of rocking, laying down with your baby, or even gently stroking his back—he will rely on the rocking, closeness to you, or stroking to help his transition to sleep. Whatever stimulation he has relied on to fall asleep at regular times will be required in order for him to fall asleep in the middle of the night.

If you teach your baby to fall asleep without your physical assistance, he will have learned to make the transition alone in less than one week. Falling asleep on his own is a valuable skill that he will use for years to come. He may use a transition object like a blanket or a teddy bear or he may suck on his hand or hold his blanket a certain way, but he'll be able to do it alone. One word of caution—don't repair your child's transition object if it gets ripped or torn or full of holes. Over years of use, these objects are designed to self-destruct. If you repair it, the blanket or teddy bear can be used as a transition object long after it's no longer necessary and long after it's socially appropriate. If you just wash the object and otherwise leave it alone, it will gradually self-destruct.

Breast-feeding

Many people assume that any woman can breast-feed a baby. However, it isn't as easy as you might think. Many factors are involved in the decision to breast-feed or bottle-feed. Most physicians and even the baby formula manufacturers recommend that mothers breast-feed if they can do so successfully. But breast-feeding is not something that comes naturally. An expectant mother who wishes to breast-feed should prepare for the process prior to the birth of the baby.

One of the most important preparation steps in breast-feeding is finding a good coach. No single factor plays a greater role in determining the success of breast-feeding than choosing a person to whom the mother can turn for support, guidance, and education. Ask your pediatrician for the name of someone who can be your support person. Ideally, this person should be a woman who has coached many other mothers to breast-feed successfully; if this person has breast-fed her own baby, she may be more empathetic. If your coach makes you feel the least bit guilty or uncomfortable, change coaches and find a new one.

Plan to meet with your coach at least one month before your expected delivery date. Some conditions, such as inverted nipples, can be treated before breast-feeding commences. Many hospitals have lactation centers that give mothers good, sound advice on breast-feeding. Some of the centers have a telephone hot line that you can use when you have questions or concerns.

Feeding Your Infant

Just as many people think that breast-feeding comes naturally to the mother, many people think that feeding solid foods to a baby is easy. You can ease the transition from breast- or bottle-feeding to feeding solid foods by following several suggestions. These suggestions were originally made by Dr. Jack Finney, a pediatric psychologist from Virginia.

1. The best single indicator of how well your baby is eating is his weight gain. Your baby should be weighed at regular intervals at your baby's pediatrician's office. It's important that your baby be weighed by the same scale each time to avoid false readings due to scale differences. Generally, do not weigh your baby more than once a month, unless asked to weight her more frequently by her doctor.

2. Feed only breast milk or infant formula to infants under the age of four months. Don't be overwhelmed by the number of formulas on the market today; start using the formula recommended by your baby's pediatrician. Do not change from one formula to another before talking to the pediatrician. Formula preparations can meet a wide variety of infant nutritional needs. For mothers who choose to bottle feed, the formulas that are marketed today are truly the next best thing to mother's milk. Do not offer supplemental feedings of water or juice until your baby is nursing well from your breast or from a bottle. Water and juice are very low in calories and can interfere with regular feedings.

3. When your infant is four to six months old, you can begin introducing solid foods. Start with an iron-fortified infant cereal. At first, solid foods should be offered to your infant for the purpose of giving him practice with new tastes, new textures, and a new way of eating. At this point, your infant will continue to get all nutritional needs from breast- or bottle-feedings.

4. In the beginning, when you introduce solid foods, do not expect your baby to swallow much cereal. Rather, expect him to play with the cereal. He will spend some time chewing it and some time spitting it out. You baby will take bites, but his tongue movements will push the food out of his mouth. This is

normal. It takes a while for babies to learn how to keep food in their mouth. Have patience.

5. Start introducing foods with only one new food at a time. Feed your baby the new food for three or four days before introducing another new food to ensure that he doesn't have an allergic reaction to the food. Vomiting, diarrhea, skin rash, and gas are possible signs that the food does not agree with your baby. If he has a reaction to the food, do not serve that food again for a few months.

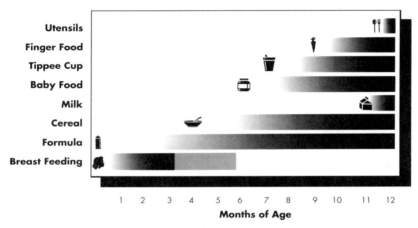

6. When your baby refuses numerous times to eat a food, wait for about two weeks before offering that food again. For example, if you offer your baby carrots and he spits the food out at every bite, wait two weeks before offering carrots again. If he still refuses, try putting a small bite of carrot with a bite of his favorite food. If he eats it, gradually add more carrot to the favorite food. Don't expect your baby to eat all foods, however. As long as he eats a few selections from the major food groups (cereal, fruit, vegetable, dairy, and protein), your baby will have a balanced diet.

7. Babies often gag when new foods are introduced. New tastes and textures can make your baby gag. If you are feeding a lumpy food, try to make the lumps smoother and try to feed

him smaller bites. If the food has a new taste, combine a few bites of the new food with a favorite food to get your baby accustomed to the new taste. If your baby gags toward the end of the meal, he is probably full and you should end the meal.

8. Babies sometimes spit up or vomit at meals if they eat too fast or eat too much. Clean up the mess as matter-of-factly as possible. If your baby doesn't seem to be sick and still is hungry, offer him a few bites more.

9. Most babies want to hold a cup and finger foods from six to nine months of age. After your baby has eaten the major foods for each meal, give him time to practice with finger foods toward the end of the meal. When you baby begins to hold a cup and finger foods, he will spill liquids and smear food all over his face and arms, on the table and high chair, and on the floor. Dropping cups, spoons, and food becomes a favorite game for many babies.

10. Do not let your baby self-feed finger foods until eating solid foods is well established. This could take a couple of months. Initially, begin the meal with you feeding your baby, then allow self-feeding only at the end of a meal.

11. Snacks will fill up your baby. Keep between-meal snacks to a minimum. Try to avoid snacks within 90 minutes of the next scheduled meal. Give water and juice between meals and bottle feedings to satisfy his thirst, especially during hot weather. On days when your baby doesn't seem to eat very well, review the snacks you fed him; too many snacks may result in poor eating at meals.

Keep mealtimes safe. Use straps to keep your baby in his infant seat or high chair. Do not put an infant seat on the table; you can put it on the floor and feed your baby there. You do not want him to fall. Never leave your baby alone while he is eating.

Do not heat the baby bottle in a microwave oven and be extremely careful about microwaving baby food. A microwave oven heats foods very unevenly; the food may seem cool to the touch, but it could have hot spots and your baby's mouth could be burned by the hot food. If you insist on using a microwave oven, always let the food sit for several minutes after heating it and always mix it thoroughly before and after cooking it.

Do not allow your baby to eat peanuts, raisins, pieces of hot dogs, or any other small-sized food. These foods could cause your baby to choke easily.

You should be relaxed when you are introducing solid foods to your baby. He needs time to become accustomed to the new tastes and textures of the foods and to the new way of eating these foods. Don't get upset about the faces that your baby may make or the sounds that he may utter when he is trying out these new foods. Rather, enjoy watching her reaction; some of the faces that babies can make when they are introduced to a food for the first time are unforgettable.

Do not rush through mealtimes. Rushing makes mealtime unpleasant for both you and your baby.

Your baby will become distracted during mealtime. He will turn his head when he hears noises, people talking, and telephones ringing. When you are feeding him, wait for him to turn his head back to you before offering him another bite of food. You can talk to your baby to get his attention. When your baby cries or turns away from you, turn your body away from him briefly (about five or ten seconds) and then offer him another bite of food. Babies often cry at the beginning of a meal when they are very hungry and they often calm down after several bites of food. End the meal if your baby is really fussy or if he is playing with the food and not trying to eat it. When your baby starts to fuss or play, it probably means that he has had enough to eat. Don't start a battle with your baby over food. You can't win food battles!

Provide your baby with a lot of soothing, physical contactduring meals. Talk to your baby frequently, but try to keep from jabbering throughout the meal. Use touch to let your child know that mealtime is a special time. Remember that mealtimes can be pleasant times to nurture and interact with your baby.

Mealtime is going to be a very messy time. Expect every meal to result in a mess. Use a plastic-backed bib on your baby. Bibs with sleeves help keep your baby's shirt sleeves cleaner, but expect him to learn quickly how to get food on his clothing, even if he's wearing a bib! He will learn how to get food on himself, on you, and on the floor. When he begins to hold a cup, grab a spoon, and practice with finger foods, the mess will be worse. You can spread newspapers or a sheet on the floor around the area where you feed your baby to make cleaning up after the meal easier. A small, portable vacuum cleaner might be handy for cleaning up the mess.

Always try to keep in mind that your baby is learning eating skills and social skills that he will use the rest of his life. Try to make your mealtimes the kind of mealtime that you want him to remember.

Night Feedings

Most new parents expect to feed their newborns at night, but many parents have no idea of how many times they will have to feed their baby every night or for how long they'll have to continue the night feedings. Many years ago, parents placed their newborns on very rigid schedules, waking their babies at at rigid intervals at night to feed them. Later, doctors recommended that babies be fed only when they were hungry, thus letting the babies themselves determine their own schedule. More recently, doctors recommend a compromise between these two approaches. While you are in the hospital, you can be fairly certain that your baby will awaken during the night and he'll either wake you up if he's in your room or the nurses will bring him to your room when he wakes up. Eventually your baby will begin sleeping through the night. The age at which this happens varies a great deal, from one or two weeks old to up to eighteen or twenty-four months old. Usually parents whose baby sleeps through the night within the first month of life are lucky; however, the ones who feed their baby during the night well into the baby's third or fourth year must enjoy getting up in the middle of the night to feed their baby. The average parent most likely does not want to get up at night for four years to feed the baby, particularly if the night feedings aren't essential to the baby's health or development.

If you want to reduce the number of months with night feedings, there are a couple of things that you can try. Several of these points were originally made by Dr. Barton Schmitt, a pediatrician from Denver who works a lot with parents and their newborns.

Don't let your baby sleep for more than three hours at a time. Some babies get their days and nights mixed up and play real havoc with your schedule. Awaken your baby gently, perhaps by rubbing his back and talking to him softly. When some babies wake up they are cute and cuddly, while others are a little more disagreeable. Don't try to feed your baby until he is completely awake. If you start feeding him too soon, he will just fall asleep while you are feeding him and will wake up hungry a short time later.

During the day it is a good idea to keep your baby busy. You can put him in his feeding chair and place him on the floor near you while you are catching up on paperwork, reading, or doing chores. When you talk to him, ask him questions and generally pay attention to him so he will be more likely to stay awake. If you keep his sleeping during the day down to three-hour segments, then you will be encouraging him to sleep longer during the night.

Don't feed your baby if he has been fed within the last two-and-one-half hours. Mothers who breast-feed their baby every two hours, around the clock, can end up resenting their baby. What starts out as a good intention on the mothers' parts turns out mothers who are fed up with their baby.

Many parents wonder whether their baby is getting enough to eat, particularly when he is breast-fed. If your baby is gaining weight on schedule, then he is getting enough to eat. Some doctors say that breast-fed babies are much less likely to become obese later in life, because these babies are more likely to stop sucking when they have had enough to eat. If you worry about your baby's food intake, ask the pediatrician. Don't begin offering more food automatically.

Night feedings should be brief and boring. The only reason for feeding at night is so your baby can eat. You will know when your baby is awake because he will cry. When you hear him crying, check his diaper. Keep the lights off, the music off, and be quiet. You should be able to love your baby, cuddle him, and feed him without talking. The only light that you will need is the light from the hallway or an adjacent room. When you are finished feeding your baby, you can rock him gently for a little while if he needs to burp, but then place him gently back into his crib or bassinet. Do not get into the habit of waiting until he is asleep before putting him back to bed; always try to put him to bed awake. That way he will learn how to relax in his bed and go to sleep. Parents should not hold their baby after every feeding until he falls asleep and then place him ever so gently back into his crib. If you do this, you will create bedtime problems; your baby cannot go to sleep without being in your arms.

Don't let your baby fall asleep in your bed and don't fall asleep in your baby's bed. It is not a good idea to feed your baby in your bed. If he becomes accustomed to eating and sleeping in your bed, you may have a difficult time getting him to stop. On the other hand, if he learns to fall asleep easily in his own bed, you can always take him into your bed occasionally without fearing that you will undo all the effort that you put into teaching him to fall asleep alone. If you are breast-feeding, Dad can be a big help during occasional night feedings by getting up when the baby cries, checking the baby's diaper, and bringing him to Mom to feed. After the feeding is over, Dad can take the baby back to his room, check his diaper again, and put him back to bed.

If you are breast-feeding, try offering breast milk in a bottle once a week so your baby will learn to accept bottle-feedings. If your baby will accept a bottle, you will be able to go out of the house to a movie, dinner, or a friend's house, and you won't have to worry whether your baby will eat. It's a good idea for the mother to the baby offer these feedings initially, because he is less likely to fuss if the bottled breast milk is coming from his Mom. Don't treat the feeding any differently. Make it as normal for you as possible, with the singular exception that the milk is in a bottle. Later, Dad or another caregiver can feed breast milk from a bottle. When your baby accepts breast milk from a bottle, Mom will be able to be away from the baby beyond the next feeding time without having to worry.

onding

Bonding refers to the intense, close attachment that a mother or father and the baby feel for each other after they get to know each other. Many parents have read and heard a great deal about the importance of bonding with their infant. Some "experts" make bonding sound so simple that it resembles some type of epoxy resin—just put the epoxy on the newborn's lips, place her on Mother's breast, and, bingo, they are bonded. Fortunately, bonding isn't that simple.

Parents develop a very close bond with their new infant over the first couple of days or weeks. The bonding is fostered by having close physical contact with your infant during that time. The easiest way to have that close contact is to be responsible for the daily caregiving your infant receives. Every time you finish a caregiving task, spend a couple of minutes holding

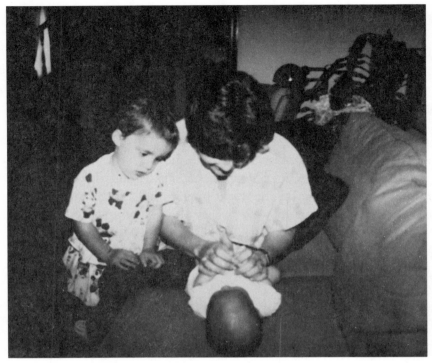

Touching, talking, and bonding

your infant, cuddling her, and physically interacting with her by checking out her hands and feet or stroking her head. Talk softly to her while you are doing the caregiving task and while you are interacting with her after the task is completed. Over time, what happens begins to feel almost like magic. You actually will begin to develop an inner glow when you are close to your baby, or even thinking about her.

Physical Contact

Most new parents touch their infants all of the time; however, as children grow, develop, and mature, fewer times are available when you can or need to touch them. Yet, there is nothing that will calm a child or that is more appreciated by a child than physical contact. Many times present themselves when you can gently pat your child on the leg, head, or arm to let him know that you love him. Whether you are in a car, watching TV at home, or eating in a restaurant, touching tells your child that you care.

Some babies will act startled or surprised when you touch them; a baby who acts this way usually hasn't been touched enough. Each touch only needs to last one or two seconds, and you don't have to say a word.

Although caregiving requires less touching as babies get older, touching is still important. Frequent, brief, nonverbal touching should be continued until your child is well into ado-lescence. There is no other way to convey a sense of love and caring. In addition to all caregiving activities, try to touch your child fifty times a day without saying anything. Over the years the touches will change, but the message that "I love you" will never change.

Living with a New Baby

When you first bring your baby home from the hospital, it's exciting just to know that you have your own baby. It won't take you long to figure out that infants are totally dependent on you for their care. You will have to learn to adapt to their dependency. Otherwise, you may end up getting so tied down that you actually find yourself resenting your infant. During the times that your infant is awake, much of your effort will be directed at caregiving. However, after your infant reaches two or three months of age, you will find increasing amounts of time during the day when he is awake but you are not administering to his basic needs. Certainly, some of this time can be spent reading to him, talking to him, or playing with him. But even that can get tiring after a month or two. Besides, parents deserve some time to themselves.

Parent's Bath and Shower Time

Parents often try to take their baths or showers before their baby awakens, during his naptime, or after he is in bed for the night. If these times are convenient for you, then you have no problem. However, you can take a bath or a shower when your baby is awake. All you need to do is place your baby in an infant carrier and place it on the bathroom floor, so that he can see you and so that you don't have to worry about him falling out or getting hurt. While you are in the bathtub or shower you can talk to him. You can ask him questions or tell him what you are doing. What you want to do is maintain his attention and let him know that you care about him. Of course, if he should become interested in something like his hand or toes, let him explore and satisfy his curiosity.

Playpens

For a number of years, playpens were not in vogue. Some people thought that only parents who didn't like their infant used playpens. That assumption is not very realistic. A playpen is very practical when you have to vacuum the floor, work on the car, or do any kind of job in which it is difficult to keep an eye on your baby or it is unsafe to have your baby near you. If you start using a playpen when your baby is very little and use it regularly for short periods of time, your baby will learn to entertain herself whenever she is placed in it. Using a playpen is hard for nervous mothers and fathers to do. If they put their baby in a playpen and she fusses and doesn't quiet down after about one minute, they conclude that she doesn't like the playpen. That is nonsense. Your baby cannot dislike the playpen

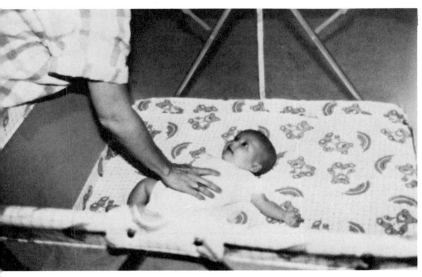

Interacting with the baby in a playpen

the first time that you put her in it. Give her a month or two to get used to being in it and you will find that she goes right to her favorite toys when she gets placed in the playpen.

Infant Feeding Chairs

Your infant will enjoy sitting in his infant feeding chair, especially if you are going to be in one room for a long length of time. A feeding chair works well when you are in the study, in the kitchen, or in the bathroom. Place your infant in the chair and put it on the floor so that he can see what you are doing and you can talk to him, but put it someplace where you don't have to step over him all the time. As he becomes accustomed to your routines, you may find that he will enjoy "visiting" with you as you go about your tasks.

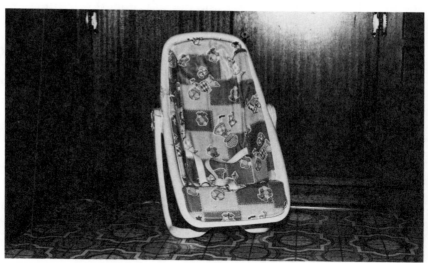

An infant feeding chair

Cloth Infant Carriers

Some parents like to carry their infant in a little cloth pouch that hangs around the parent's neck. It supports the infant by holding her against the parent's chest or abdomen.

Some parents enjoy doing errands with their infant securely held in front of them. Some doctors recommend carrying your baby in a cloth carrier for three hours a day if your baby has colic. Sometimes carrying her this way will help decrease her crying. However, carrying your baby in a pouch can be risky— you could trip and fall forward, with your weight on the baby. You'll have to decide for yourself if you want to use one of these devices.

Holding baby in a cloth infant carrier

Backpacks to Carry Infants

Backpacks are available in which to carry your infant. They are made of cloth and have a metal frame on the two sides to keep their shape and to support the baby. In a backpack, your baby will be riding on your back, facing forward. Some parents find these to be very comfortable and like to use them while shopping or going for walks. Most newborns are too small to put them in one of these carriers, but they work well after the baby is is big enough to sit in the backpack.

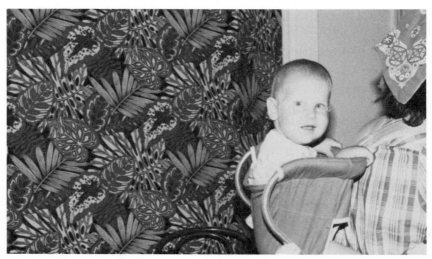

Riding in a backpack

Baby Swings

A baby swing is invaluable to have for your new baby. Baby swings come in two basic styles: an A-frame style that has a wind-up motor for the swing and a hanging style that hooks over the door frame and is free-swinging. The rhythm of the swing helps to console many babies. Many babies who can't be comforted in any other way often will drift off to sleep once they get in the swing. This is not a problem—let them sleep right in the swing.

Talking to Your Baby

Long before your baby utters her first word, you should talk to her about her surroundings. When she is able to hold up her head by herself (usually by one or two months of age), you can carry her around with you, in your arms, in her carrier, or in her backpack. You can carry her around the house, the store, or the park while talking to her. You will find that you enjoy talking with her as you go about your routines. Point out things to her, telling her what they are and what they do. Many parents interact with their baby by holding her and pointing to parts of their own body like the eyes, ears, or nose and telling her what each one is as they point to it.

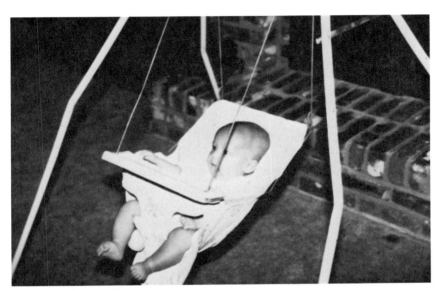

Swinging in a swing

Baby-sitters

Most new mothers and fathers find it very difficult to be separated from their infant. Parents often feel very uncomfortable about leaving their baby and entrusting her care to another person. Before you are faced with an emergency situation and are forced to leave your baby with a baby-sitter, you should get used to having another caregiver stay with your baby. A good way to get accustomed to the idea of a baby-sitter is to have the baby-sitter come to your home and take care of your baby, but, instead of you leaving your home, stay in your bedroom where you can listen to what's going on and assure yourself that your baby will be happy and cared for.

Remember that baby-sitters are paid employees, much like any other employee who is hired to perform a service for you. You should interview prospective baby-sitters and learn about their previous caregiving experiences. Watch the prospective baby-sitter interact with your baby. Ask for references and check them out.

To ease your anxiety and to make baby-sitting easier for your employee, a baby-sitting handout can be prepared. This handout should include important details about your house and your family. For example, if you were to become incapacitated in any way while your baby is in the care of a baby-sitter, from being stuck in an elevator, to being involved in an automobile accident, to becoming ill on the way home, your baby-sitter must know whom to contact for emergencies. In the handout, you should describe your house and the rules that are in effect when the baby-sitter is in charge. The handout should include such items as how to find the water pipe shut-off in the basement, the names and phone numbers of friends and family members who could be contacted in case of an emergency, and instructions for power outages. Some people may think that it is silly to make such elaborate preparations; however, your anxiety will be less if you know that your sitter is well informed about your home and family.

In the back of this book is a sample of a baby-sitting handout that you can copy for your use. An example of a completed handout is also shown.

Separation Anxiety

Infants usually do not get upset when one of their parents puts them in their crib or hands them to another person. Generally, the babies who fuss and cry when their parents leave

Showing good separation skills

them are reacting to their parents and not to the actual separation. Some parents are so sad that their voices choke up and they get tears in their eyes because they are leaving their baby for a short time. Babies sense this type of reaction and respond to it by fussing more when they know that Mom or Dad is leaving.

The first few times that you leave your child with a baby-sitter or at a day-care center may be very emotional for you. Try to treat these separations in a matter-of-fact manner. If your child learns separation skills, then these times will not be hard for you or your child. Plan ahead prior to the separations so that you can separate quickly. Have your child's belongings together and ready to go. Don't discuss the separation with your child before it occurs. If you find that separation from your child is very difficult for you, then practice separating from her more often. Generally, the best treatment for separation anxiety is to keep separating until the anxiety diminishes. Arrange to leave your child at a friend's or relative's house several times a week until you become good at separating.

Owner Assistance

No experience has greater potential for bringing joy and fulfillment to your life than raising a child. The intensity of emotions that your children evoke in you is unlike anything else. Most parents have no training in child rearing when their first baby is born. The intent of this book is to give you an idea of what you can expect after your baby is born. It should help you to tackle each day separately, without becoming too serious about any one thing that your baby does.

Evaluating Maturity

As you acquire more knowledge about babies and the way they normally act and react to things, you can adjust your life more easily to include a baby. To show you how your infant reacts to his environment, the *Infant Progress Monitor* is included in the back of this book to help you follow your baby's maturity and development. You should answer the questions in the *Infant Progress Monitor* once a week for at least the first two months of your baby's life. There are no right or wrong responses to the *Infant Progress Monitor*. It is a tool to help you become familiar with your baby. Some of your baby's responses that seem crude and jerky at first will become much smoother in that two-month period of time. The *Infant Progress Monitor* is based on a questionnaire that was developed by Dr. Tiffany Field, a psychologist in Florida.

Problem-solving

Your peace of mind is important to you and your baby. Usually, you will be able to manage any problems you have

with your baby by yourself. However, despite your best efforts, there will be times when you feel you cannot handle your concerns with help. This is a normal feeling for all parents and when you feel this way, there are several steps to follow.

Step one. Discuss your problem with a successful parent. A successful parent may be one of your parents, a relative, or a neighbor—someone who has raised a child who generally behaves in an acceptable manner most of the time. This step automatically excludes well-intentioned individuals who don't know what you are talking about because they either have never experienced what you are going through, or they have experienced it but not handle it very well.

Step two. Make an appointment to discuss your concerns with your baby's doctor or nurse. Ask for an appointment that is long enough so you can discuss the problem to your satisfaction. You may be charged a little bit more for the appointment than you would for a routine well-baby visit because the appointment may last a longer time. Ask the office receptionist which days are the least congested, so that scheduling extra time will not pose any problems. If the receptionist tells you that the doctor or nurse does not schedule such appointments, then proceed to step three.

Prior to going to the appointment, plan to organize your thoughts; write down your concerns and what you expect to be accomplished from this appointment. Take pen and paper with you to the appointment so that you can write down the recommendations. Read what you wrote down with the doctor or nurse to ensure that you recorded the correct information. You may find that you have nothing written down at the end of the appointment. All you may have needed was a sympathetic ear or someone to help you sort your thoughts. Maybe the doctor or nurse had little to say. If you were unable to get satisfactory help from this appointment, perhaps you should go elsewhere the next time you have an important question.

Step three. If you feel you and your baby need additional help, go to a teaching hospital or university and locate a department that has professionals who specialize in small children with a variety of problems. Carefully check the department you select and make sure the department treats normal infants and young children for normal problems. Generally, this type of assistance can be found in a department of pediatrics or in a department of child development. Typically, this type of assistance is not found in a mental health center or in a psychiatry department. Most mental health practitioners who deal with problems of mental or emotional adjustment do not provide services for normal children with normal problems. You need to talk to a professional who deals with young, normal children all the time, not one who will "do you a favor" and see your baby.

If the professional you see recommends that some psychological tests on your baby be performed, think twice. No psychological tests can measure adequately the adjustment of normal infants. However, it is appropriate to test the developmental progress of infants, such as the age at which he sat up or walked. The most widely used of these tests is the Denver Developmental Screening Test and it can be administered in the pediatrician's office in about twenty minutes, usually at little expense to you.

If the professional wants your baby to be admitted to a hospital for a series of tests, ask yourself some questions. Do you think the reason your baby is doing or is not doing something because of a physical condition? If so, did you give the professional a complete history of the problem prior to the recommendation of hospital admission? Unless your baby is critically ill, the professional should schedule an office appointment for you and your baby before deciding to admit your baby to a hospital.

Additional Reading

If you are interested in reading additional books, several good ones are available. They are written by knowledgeable individuals and should be available in most major bookstores.

Infants & Mothers: Differences in Development (revised edition), by Dr. T. Berry Brazelton, covers the first year of life. Dr. Brazelton describes the characteristics of an average baby, a quiet baby, and an active baby for each month for the first twelve months of life. Although your baby may not be similar to the ones described by Dr. Brazelton, the information contained in the book is helpful.

Dr. Spock's Baby & Child Care, by Dr. Benjamin Spock and Michael Rothenberg is one of the biggest-selling books on child care. The book contains more information than most other books of this type. It is a good book to have available in your home so that you can look up answers to your questions easier. Although more recent editions have been published, the 1976 edition seems to be the most comprehensive.

Little People: Guidelines for Commonsense Child Rearing (third edition), by Dr. Edward Christophersen, is a practical guide to living with a young child. In the book, concrete suggestions are made to help make the time that parents spend with their children more enjoyable.

Your Child's Health: A Pediatric Guide for Parents, by Dr. Barton D. Schmitt, is one of the most useful and authoritative pediatric guidebooks currently available for parents.

Infant Progress Monitor

1. When you play with your baby, is he usually:
    a) sleepy
    b) alert
    c) upset

2. How much do you have to stimulate your baby to get him to look at you?
    a) not very much
    b) a fair amount
    c) a lot

3. When your baby is upset, what does he do to quiet himself?
    a) brings his hand to his mouth
    b) sucks with nothing in his mouth
    c) looks at you

4. Try talking to your baby while holding your face about one foot away from his face and then slowly move your face to one side and then to the other as you continue talking. When you do this, your baby:
    a) doesn't look at you
    b) becomes quiet and looks at you
    c) follows your face to each side with his head and eyes
    d) follows your face with his head and eyes, up and down and to each side

5. Now try the same thing, only move your face without talking. When you do this your baby:
    a) doesn't look at you
    b) becomes quiet
    c) follows your face with his head and eyes
    d) follows your face with his head and eyes, up and down and to each side

6. Try talking to your baby from one side of her head, then from the other. When you do this he:
    a) has no reaction or he blinks
    b) becomes quiet
    c) turns his eyes and head to your voice once or twice
    d) turns his eyes and head to your voice more than two times

7. Now try holding a colorful toy or some shiny object in front of your baby's face and then move it slowly to one side of his head and then up and down in front of his face. When you do this he:
    a) doesn't look at the toy
    b) becomes quiet and looks at the toy
    c) follows the toy you are moving with his head and eyes
    d) follows the toy you are moving with his head and eyes, up and down and to each side

8. Try shaking a rattle on one side of your baby's head and then the other side. When you do this he:
    a) has no reaction or he blinks
    b) becomes quiet
    c) turns his eyes and head to the rattle once or twice
    d) turns his eyes and head to the rattle more than two times

9. When you did the above things with your baby he usually:
    a) paid little attention to you or the toy
    b) had short periods of watching you or the toy
    c) watched you or the toy for a fairly long time
    d) paid attention most of the time

10. When your baby moves his arms the movements are:
    a) jerky most of the time
    b) jerky some of the time
    c) smooth some of the time
    d) smooth most of the time

11. When you pick up your baby and hold him in a rocking position:
    a) he often swings his arms and kicks his legs and squirms a lot
    b) he's like a sack of flour in your arms
    c) he relaxes and nestles his head in your arms
    d) he moves his face toward you and reaches his hands out to grab your clothing

12. When your baby is crying very hard:
    a) nothing seems to quiet him
    b) only a pacifier will quiet him
    c) holding and rocking him will quiet him
    d) talking to him and holding your hand on his stomach quiets him

13. How would you describe your baby most of the time?
    a) very sleepy
    b) awake a lot of the time and quiet
    c) cries occasionally but is easily quieted
    d) cries a lot and is difficult to quiet

14. Please circle the activities which upset your baby:
    a) changing his diaper
    b) undressing or dressing him
    c) putting him back in the bassinet
    d) laying him on his stomach

15. How active is your baby?
    a) not very active
    b) somewhat active
    c) quite active
    d) very active

16. When your baby is crying, how successful is he at quieting himself?
    a) he cannot quiet herself
    b) he makes several attempts to quiet himself but is usually unsuccessful
    c) he has many brief successes at quieting himself
    d) he often quiets himself for long periods of time

17. How would you describe your baby's hand-to-mouth activity?
    a) he makes no attempt to bring his hands to his mouth
    b) he often brings his hand next to his mouth
    c) he sometimes puts his fist or fingers in his mouth
    d) he sometimes sucks on his fist or fingers for as long as 15 minutes at a time

18. How many times has your baby looked like he was smiling at you?

Adapted from Mother's Assessment of the Behavior of Her Infant (MABI), by Tiffany M. Field, 1978, with permission.

Baby-sitting for the _White's_

Emergency Number (Police/Fire) _911_
Doctor _Brown - 757 - 1234_
Next-door Neighbor _Joe and Mary Jones 321-1111_
Nearest Relative _Sue and Bill White 493-6554_
Husband's Work _ABC Co. 677-4432_
Wife's Work _United Inc. 455-7522_
Electric Company _471-7000_
Gas Company _561- 2200_
We will be at _Jerry's Restaurant 341·6322_

If a crisis occurs, attempt to get in touch with us first.

Locks _Backdoor lock uses a key on the inside. The key hangs on the wall by door._
Lights _The outside lights go on automatically at dusk. Please leave them on._
Fire Extinguisher _Located in the front hall closet. There's a flashlight next to it._
Power Failure _If power goes off, an emergency light in family room goes on automatically._
Visitors _Do not answer the door. Don't let anyone in the house for any reason._
Smoke Detector _If it goes off, get the kids, go to the neighbor's house, call 911, then call us._
Telephone _Answer the phone, and always tell the caller you don't know when we'll be home_
Fireplace _Don't start a fire in the fireplace._

Water Crisis _The main water valve is in the basement to the right of stairs. Directions are by the valve._
Food _You are welcome to eat any food that we have_
Freezer _If the buzzer sounds, the freezer has shut off. Don't open freezer. Call us._

Baby-sitting for the _____

Emergency Number (Police/Fire) _____
Doctor _____
Next-door Neighbor _____
Nearest Relative _____
Husband's Work _____
Wife's Work _____
Electric Company _____
Gas Company _____
We will be at _____

If a crisis occurs, attempt to get in touch with us first.

Locks _____

Lights _____

Fire Extinguisher _____

Power Failure _____

Visitors _____

Smoke Detector _____

Telephone _____

Fireplace _____

Water Crisis _____

Food _____

Freezer _____

About the Author

Dr. Edward R. Christophersen is a clinical psychologist at The Children's Mercy Hospital in Kansas City, Missouri, where he is also Chief of the Behavioral Sciences Section.

For over fifteen years, Dr. Christophersen has lectured on child rearing to prenatal classes and seminars on parenting. He is a frequent lecturer throughout the United States and Canada, addressing both professional and lay audiences. He appears frequently on radio and television programs throughout the country.

Dr. Christophersen has conducted extensive research on child-rearing practices. He is a Fellow of the American Psychological Association and is a member of the American Association for Marriage and Family Therapy. He is the author of over 100 articles appearing in professional journals and popular magazines. He is the author of another book, *Little People: Guidelines for Commonsense Child Rearing*.

Dr. Christophersen received a Ph.D. in Developmental and Child Psychology in 1970 from the University of Kansas. He lives with his wife and two children in suburban Kansas City.

The Third Edition
Little People
Thoroughly Updated and Revised

Rearing children is both the most delightful and the most trying experience most of us will ever be privileged to enjoy. It produces an overwhelming exhilaration that is difficult to explain, but impossible to get any other way. All parents have some problems with their children, yet almost every parent who has problems with a child is doing the best possible job of child rearing that he or she knows how to do. Quite simply, child rearing is something that few parents are prepared or trained for. This book is for them — parents who for the most part are doing a good job, but who want to do better.

Dr. Christophersen takes the commonsense approach that children are little people, but still people. How well children are prepared for life and how much they will enjoy life has a lot to do with how they are raised.

Catch 'Em Being Good is one of Dr. Christophersen's favorite pieces of advice. The entire book, **Little People**, is built around guidelines that will help you to encourage your child's positive behavior. The book discusses the importance of touching to support a child's emotional development and self-esteem. Dr. Christophersen's advice also comforts parents by discussing what is normal and acceptable behavior.

Little People is a positive book meant to help parents get the most out of the years they spend with the little people they bring into the world and help them grow up happy and healthy.

$$* \quad * \quad *$$

"Dr. Christophersen brings a fresh look…writes with humor and empathy."
Sun Newspapers

"Christophersen is refreshing…clear language."
Arizona Daily Star

"One of the most helpful resources…"
Salina Journal Sunflower

$$* \quad * \quad *$$

Little People is recommended by pediatricians, obstetricians, psychologists, teachers, and most of all — by parents.

ISBN 0-933701-32-2 • $9.95

ORDER DIRECT
CALL 1-800-822-8485

❏ **YES**, I want _____ copies of
Little People for **$9.95** each
plus $2 shipping.
❏ **YES**, I want _____ copies of
Baby Owner's Manual for **$6.95**
each plus $2 shipping.

Method of Payment

❏ Check to:

Westport Publishers
4050 Pennsylvania Ave.
Suite 310
Kansas City, MO 64111
for $ _____

❏ Charge my credit card
❏ Visa   ❏ MasterCard
Acct. # _____
Exp. Date _____
Signature _____

Ship to: _____
_____
_____
_____
_____

- -

ORDER DIRECT
CALL 1-800-822-8485

❏ **YES**, I want _____ copies of
Little People for **$9.95** each
plus $2 shipping.
❏ **YES**, I want _____ copies of
Baby Owner's Manual for **$6.95**
each plus $2 shipping.

Method of Payment

❏ Check to:

Westport Publishers
4050 Pennsylvania Ave.
Suite 310
Kansas City, MO 64111
for $ _____

❏ Charge my credit card
❏ Visa   ❏ MasterCard
Acct. # _____
Exp. Date _____
Signature _____

Ship to: _____
_____
_____
_____
_____

Westport Publishers
4050 Pennsylvania Ave.
Suite 310
Kansas City, MO 64111

Westport Publishers
4050 Pennsylvania Ave.
Suite 310
Kansas City, MO 64111

ORDER DIRECT
CALL 1-800-822-8485

❏ **YES**, I want _____ copies of
  Little People for **$9.95** each
  plus $2 shipping.
❏ **YES**, I want _____ copies of
  Baby Owner's Manual for **$6.95**
  each plus $2 shipping.

Method of Payment

❏ Check to:

Westport Publishers   **Ship to:** _____
4050 Pennsylvania Ave.   _____
Suite 310
Kansas City, MO 64111   _____
for $ _____   _____

❏ Charge my credit card   _____
❏ Visa   ❏ MasterCard

Acct. # _____
Exp. Date _____
Signature _____

■■■

ORDER DIRECT
CALL 1-800-822-8485

❏ **YES**, I want _____ copies of
  Little People for **$9.95** each
  plus $2 shipping.
❏ **YES**, I want _____ copies of
  Baby Owner's Manual for **$6.95**
  each plus $2 shipping.

Method of Payment

❏ Check to:

Westport Publishers   **Ship to:** _____
4050 Pennsylvania Ave.   _____
Suite 310
Kansas City, MO 64111   _____
for $ _____   _____

❏ Charge my credit card   _____
❏ Visa   ❏ MasterCard

Acct. # _____
Exp. Date _____
Signature _____

Westport Publishers
4050 Pennsylvania Ave.
Suite 310
Kansas City, MO 64111

Westport Publishers
4050 Pennsylvania Ave.
Suite 310
Kansas City, MO 64111